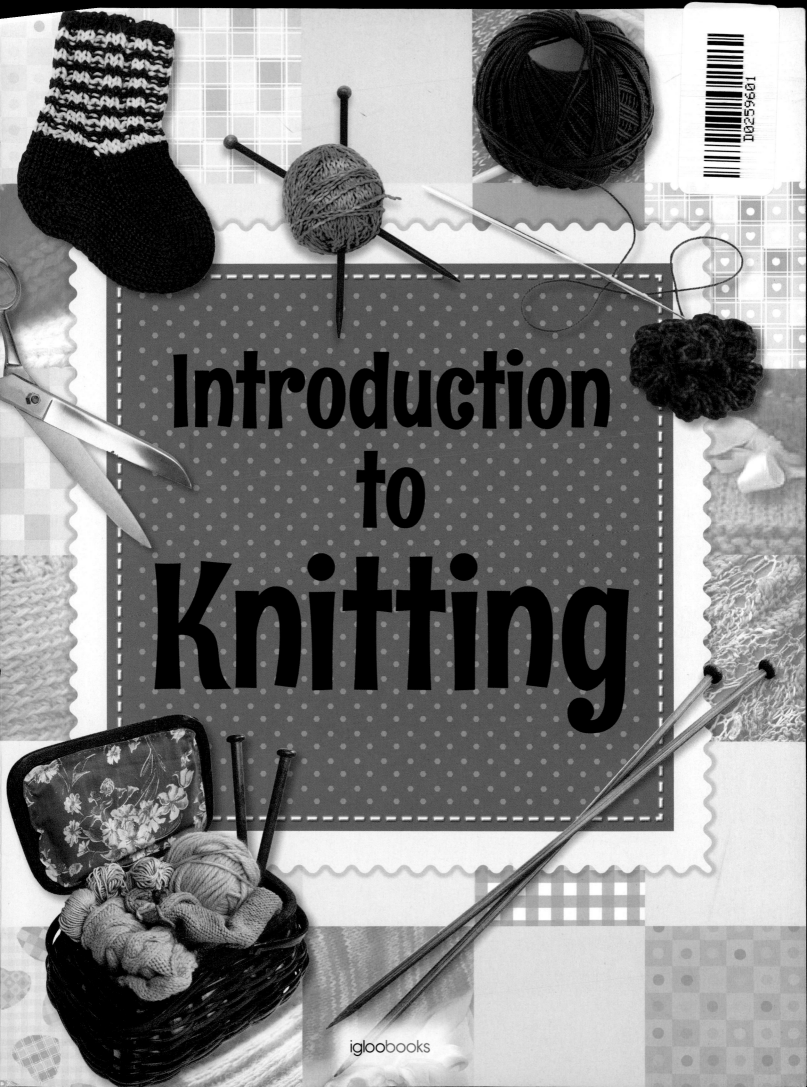

Introduction to Knitting

igloobooks

Published in 2015
by Igloo Books Ltd
Cottage Farm
Sywell
NN6 0BJ
www.igloobooks.com

Cover images © Thinkstock / Getty Images

LEO002 0715
2 4 6 8 10 9 7 5 3 1
ISBN 978-1-78440-284-6

Printed and manufactured in China

Introduction
to
Knitting

Contents

Introduction

Clothes

Accessories

Introduction

Follow the step-by-step instructions in this comprehensive how-to guide and learn to fashion your own garments and accessories using basic stitches and a drop of creativity.

LEARN TO KNIT:

The Basic Stitches

The following pages contain the basic stitches that you will need to begin knitting. Each how-to section covers a different stitch, with comprehensive step-by-step explanations and accompanying images.

Slipknot

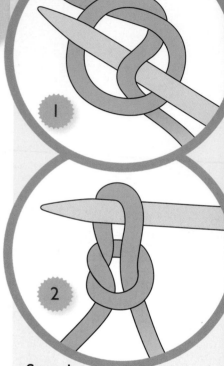

Long-tail Cast On

This uses a single needle and produces an elastic knitted edge like a row of garter stitch.

Step 1

Leaving an end about three times the length of the required cast-on, put a slipknot on the needle. Holding the yarn end in the left hand, take the left thumb under the yarn and upwards. Insert the needle in the loop just made on the thumb.

Step 2

Use the ball end of the yarn to make a knit stitch, slipping the loop off the thumb. Pull the yarn end to close the stitch up to the needle. Continue making stitches in this way.

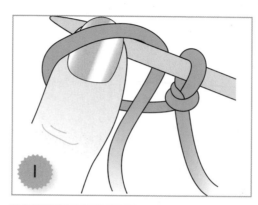

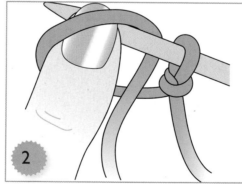

Chain Cast Off

A simple knit stitch cast off is used in most of these projects. Knit two stitches. * With the left needle, lift the first stitch over the second. Knit the next stitch. Repeat from * until one stitch remains. Break the yarn, take the end through this stitch and tighten.

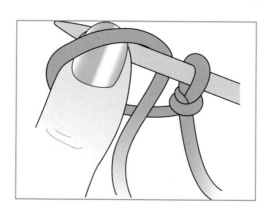

Step 1

A slipknot is the first stage of any cast on. Loop the yarn around two fingers of the left hand, the ball end on top. Dip the needle into the loop, catch the ball end of the yarn and pull it through the loop.

Step 2

Pull the ends of the yarn to tighten the knot. Tighten the ball end to bring the knot up to the needle

Ends

The end of yarn left after casting on should be a reasonable length of approx 10–30cm/4–12in so that it can be used for sewing up. The same applies to the end left after casting off.

Knit Stitch (K)

Choose to hold the yarn and needles in whichever way you feel most comfortable. To create tension in the yarn – that is, to keep it moving evenly – you will need to twist it through some fingers of the hand holding the yarn, and maybe even take it around your little finger. Continuous rows of knit stitch produce garter stitch. It does take some practice to get the stitches even so don't be discouraged, keep on practising.

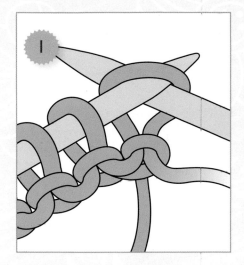

Step 1

Insert the right needle into the first stitch on the left needle. Make sure it goes from left to right into the front of the stitch.

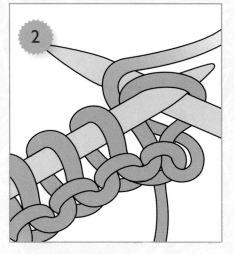

Step 2

Taking the yarn behind, bring it up and around the right needle.

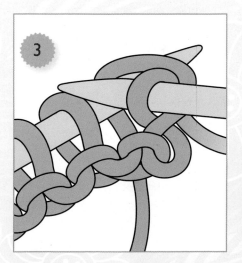

Step 3

Using the tip of the right needle, draw a loop of yarn through the stitch.

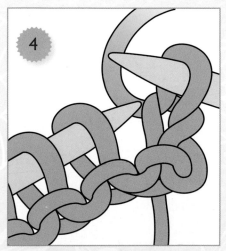

Step 4

Slip the stitch off the left needle. There is now a new stitch on the right needle.

Purl Stitch (P)

Step 1
Insert the right needle into the first stitch on the left needle. Make sure it goes into the stitch from right to left.

Step 2
Lower the tip of the right needle, taking it away from you to draw a loop of yarn through the stitch.

Step 3
Taking the yarn to the front, loop it around the right needle.

Step 4
Slip the stitch off the left needle. There is now a new stitch on the right needle.

Decreases

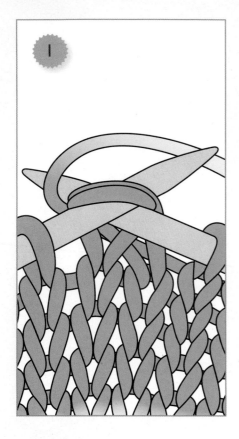

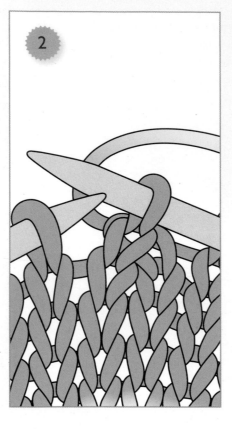

Decreases have two basic functions. They can be used to reduce the number of stitches in a row, as in armholes and necklines, and combined with increases, they can create stitch patterns.

Right-slanting single decrease (k2tog)

Knitting two stitches together makes a smooth shaping, with the second stitch lying on top of the first.

Step 1

Insert the right needle through the front of the first two stitches on the left needle, then take the yarn around the needle.

Step 2

Draw the loop through and drop the two stitches off the left needle.

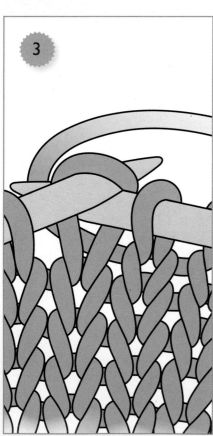

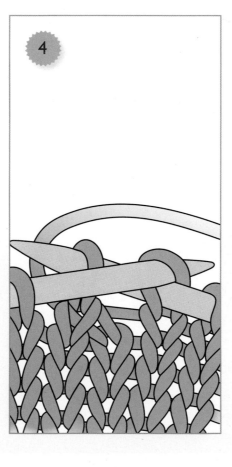

Left-slanting double decrease (sk2po)

For a double decrease that slants to the left, worked on a right-side row, you'll need to take the first stitch over a single decrease. For a similar-looking decrease worked on a wrong-side row, purl three together through the back of the loops (p3tog tbl).

Step 1

Insert the right needle knitwise through the front of the first stitch on the left needle, and slip it onto the right needle.

Step 2

Knit the next two stitches together, then lift the first stitch over as shown. To make a right-slanting double decrease, simply knit three stitches together (k3tog).

Cables

Knitting groups of stitches out of sequence creates exciting stitch patterns. Cables can be worked with two or more stitches and crossed to the front or the back.

Front cable (c4f)

The stitches in this example are knitted, and this four-stitch cable crosses at the front. A four-stitch back cable (c4b) is worked in exactly the same way, except that the cable needle is held at the back, so that the cable crosses in the opposite direction.

Step 1

Slip the first two stitches onto a cable needle and hold at the front of the work, then knit the next two stitches from the left needle.

Step 2

Knit the two stitches from the cable needle.

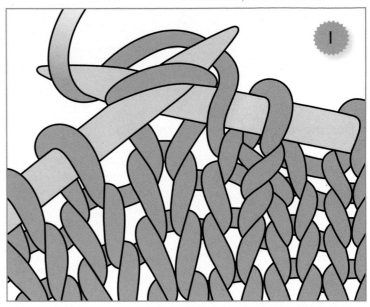

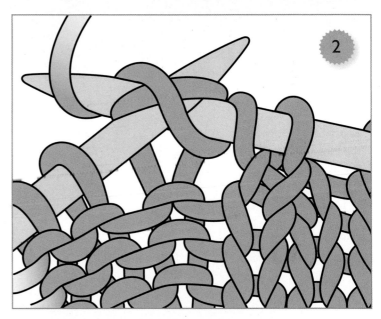

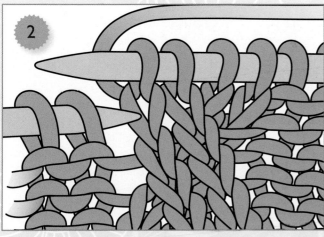

Yarn Over (YO)

It's essential to take the yarn over the needle so that the strand lies in the same direction as the other stitches. Working into this strand on the next row makes a hole, but if the strand is twisted, the hole will close up. When the stitch before a yarn over is purl, the yarn will already be at the front, ready to go over the needle.

Step 1

To make a yarn over between knit stitches, bring the yarn to the front as if to purl, then take it over the needle to knit the next stitch.

Step 2

To make a yarn over between a knit and a purl, bring the yarn to the front as if to purl, take it over the needle and bring it to the front again, ready to purl.

Increases

Here are two of the most basic methods of increasing a single stitch – bar increase and lifted strand increase.

Bar increase on a knit row (kfb)

Knitting into the front and the back of a stitch is the most common increase. It's a neat, firm increase, which makes a little bar on the right side of the work at the base of the new stitch. This makes it easy to count rows between shapings and doesn't leave a hole.

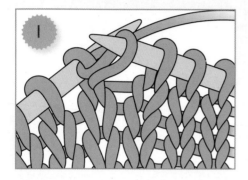

Step 1

Knit into the front of the stitch and pull the loop through, but leave the stitch on the left needle.

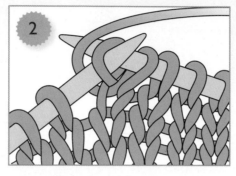

Step 2

Knit into the back of the stitch on the left needle.

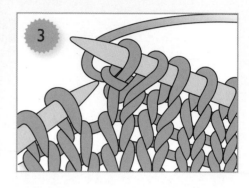

Step 3

Slip the stitch off the left needle, making two stitches on the right needle. Note that the bar of the new stitch lies on the left.

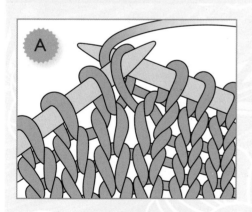

Lifted strand increase to the left (m1 or m1L)

Making a stitch from the strand between stitches is a very neat way to increase.

Picture A

From the front, insert the left needle under the strand between stitches. Make sure the strand lies on the needle in the same direction as the other stitches, then knit into the back of it.

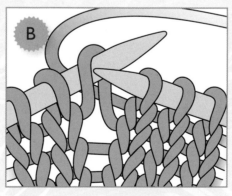

Lifted strand increase to the right (m1R)

This right-slanting increase balances exactly the lifted strand increase to the left.

Picture B

From the back, insert the left needle under the strand between the stitches. It will not lie in the same direction as the other stitches, so knit into the front of it.

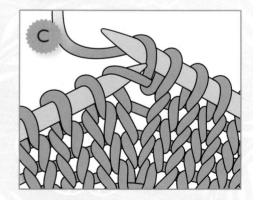

Double increase

This is one of the simplest ways to make three stitches out of one.

Picture C

Knit one stitch without slipping it off, take the yarn over the right needle from front to back then knit the same stitch again. A small but decorative hole is left in the fabric.

Twists

Twisting stitches is working two or three stitches out of sequence, but without using a cable needle. This is an easy way to create patterns where lines of stitches travel over the surface of the knitting.

Left twist (t2L)

This twist is worked on a right-side row. As the stitches change place, the first stitch lies on top and slants to the left, while the stitch behind is worked through the back of the loop.

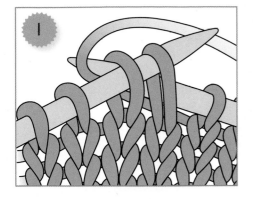 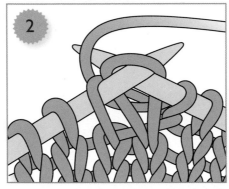 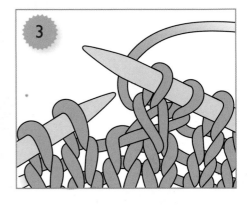

Step 1

Knit into the back of the second stitch.

Step 2

Knit into the front of the first stitch.

Step 3

Slip both stitches off the left needle together.

Right twist (t2R)

In this right-sided row twist, the second stitch lies on top and slants to the right, while the stitch behind is worked through the back of the loop.

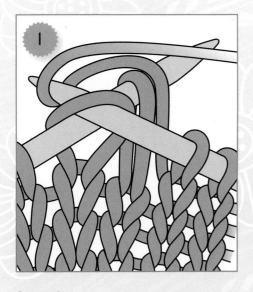 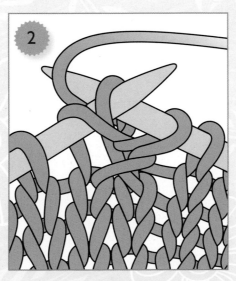 

Step 1

Knit into the front of the second stitch.

Step 2

Knit into the back of the first stitch.

Step 3

Slip both stitches off the left needle together.

Knitting Essentials

Learning the lingo, understanding needle sizes and being able to change colours are essentials that every keen knitter should know.

Knitting is an enjoyable and rewarding hobby, but sometimes it can be daunting. It may look like a world of meaningless letters and confusing numbers but by learning the lingo and becoming familiar with the tools and techniques, it will all make sense. Knitting abbreviations are one of the trickiest elements of the knitting world, but 'k2tog' does actually mean something. The list opposite will decipher the code and it will soon be second nature.

Needles come in a wide variety of sizes. They are your most vital tool so it is important that you know your 6s from your 6mm. Thin needles are required for small and fine projects whereas larger needles are used for chunkier tasks. The chart opposite will help you choose the right needle for your project. We will also guide you through the basics of changing colour for when you are ready to move on.

Changing Colour

Changing colour to create stripes is most easily done at the end of a row. First, knit all the rows that you need to, with your first colour. When you are ready to change colour, drop the old colour. Pick up the new colour by threading the beginning of the new colour through the back of the last stitch and pulling the old colour tightly, trapping the new colour. Hold both the start of the new colour and the end of the old colour together and resume knitting as normal, using the new colour. After every row, pull the end of the new colour to keep it tight, but ensure that the tension is kept even. Cut the old colour, leaving a 15cm/6in tail. Use a tapestry needle to weave the loose ends in.

Abbreviations

alt	alternate
approx	approximately
beg	beginning
CC	contrast colour
cont	continue
dec	decrease(ing)
DPN	double-pointed needle
foll	following
folls	follows
g st	garter stitch
inc	increase(ing)
k	knit
k2tog	knit 2 together
kfb	knit into front and back of st
KTS	knit the steek st
kwise	knitwise
LH	left hand
m1	make one
m1l	make one left
m1r	make one right
m1p	make one purl
MC	main colour
N1/N2	needle 1/needle 2
p	purl
p2tog	purl 2 together
patt	pattern
pm	place marker
psso	pass slipped st over
pwise	purlwise
rem	remain(ing)
rep	repeat
rnd	round
RH	right hand
RS	right side
sl1	slip 1 st
skpo	sl1, k1, pass sl st over
sm	slip marker
ssk	slip first st, slip second st, then work both together off right-hand needle
st(s)	stitch(es)
st st	stocking stitch
tbl	through back of loop/s
tog	together
w&t	wrap and turn
wyif	with yarn in front
WS	wrong side
yf	yarn forward
yo	yarn over
yon	yarn over needle
yrn	yarn round needle

Needle Conversion Chart

mm	UK	US
2.0mm	14	0
2.25mm	13	1
2.5mm	12	
2.75mm	12	2
3.0mm	11	3
3.25mm	10	3
3.5mm	9	4
3.75mm	9	5
4.0mm	8	6
4.5mm	7	7
5.0mm	6	8
5.5mm	5	9
6.0mm	4	10
6.5mm	3	10½
7.0mm	2	
7.5mm	1	
8.0mm	0	11
9.0mm	00	13
10mm	000	15

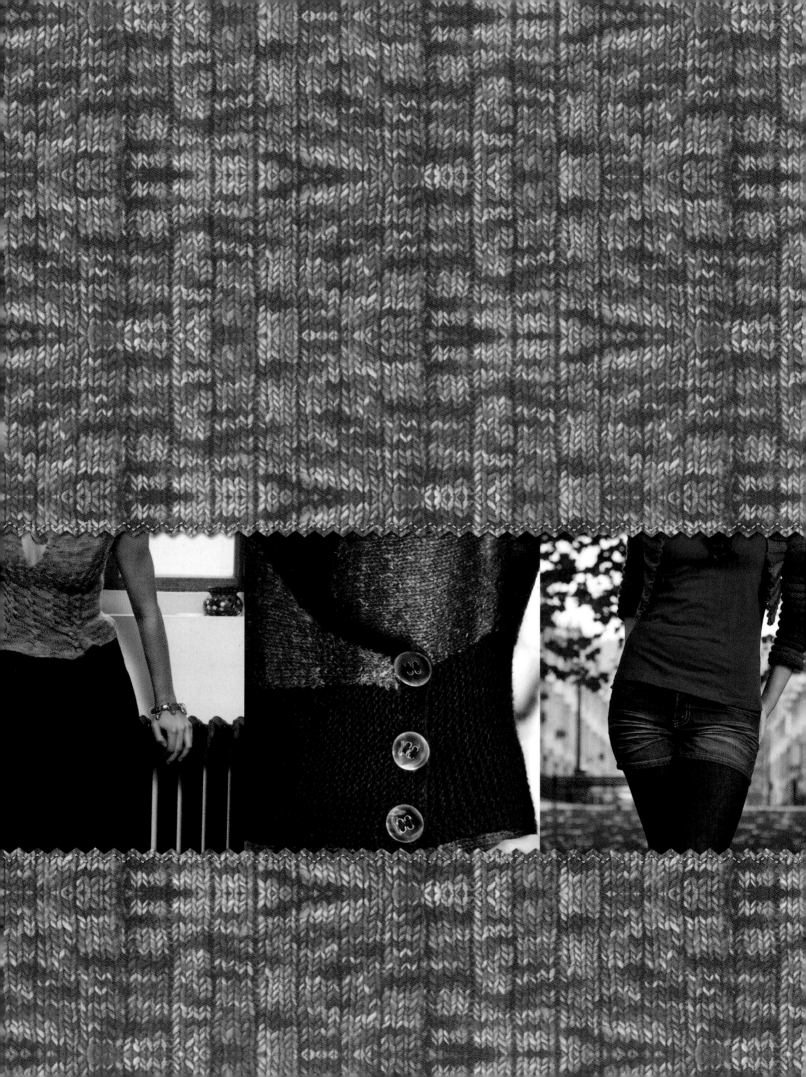

Clothes

Dive into more complex projects in this exciting clothing section and knit your very own vibrant, one-of-a-kind garments that you will want to wear time and time again.

BASIC GARMENT
Alterations

If you're wearing a sweater made just for you, shouldn't it fit perfectly? This simple guide gives you the basics to adapt any pattern to suit your shape.

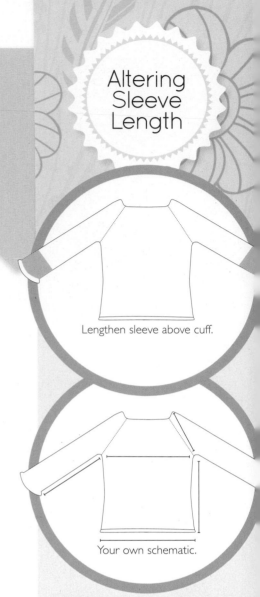

Altering Sleeve Length

Lengthen sleeve above cuff.

Your own schematic.

Knowing your own body shape is critical for knitting garments that fit you perfectly. Not every pattern that you fall in love with is going to look as good on you as it does in the magazine, so here is a brief introduction to understanding what you need to change in order to get a perfect custom fit.

Finding your ideal measurements

Find a favourite sweater or cardigan (hand-knitted or shop-bought) and lay it out on a flat surface. Grab a pencil, paper and tape measure and get ready to measure.

The key measurements to take are: length of sleeve from armpit to cuff; length from armpit to bottom of garment; length from armpit to shoulder; bust; and bottom edge of garment. Using our blank schematic (above right), record the exact measurements of these points on your favourite garment and then compare

them with the measurements given on the schematic of the garment you wish to make.

Some differences are much easier to amend than others. You also need to remember that the stitch pattern that the garment is knitted in will have an impact on how complicated it will be to alter the pattern to fit you perfectly.

Don't skip the swatch!

Before you start working out how to alter the pattern, you need to knit a tension square. This is a step that even many experienced knitters will ignore, but any designer or pattern alterer will tell you it is a critical step in ensuring that you are knitting to the exact size that the pattern is written for, as well as in understanding the drape and texture of the yarn that you are using.

Look at the pattern. If a lace or cable stitch is involved, it is best to make two swatches. If it is knitted in stocking stitch, cast on half a dozen stitches more than the pattern recommends for 10cm/4in and work until you have a square.

Measure your swatch and using our blank swatch picture (left), write down

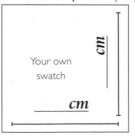

Your own swatch

cm

cm

the tension of your swatch (the number of stitches and rows per 10cm/4in square) and then check

Altering sleeve length

Sleeves that are longer or shorter than your ideal garment are probably among the easiest amendments to make. By looking at your sleeve measurement on the blank schematic, you will easily be able to see how many inches or centimetres you need to add or reduce to make it fit. Compare this with your tension square to see how those inches convert to rows, and that is how many extra or fewer rows you will need to knit. The best place to alter on a sleeve is just after the cuff stitches, before any shaping takes place. For instance, if the sleeve starts with 10 rows of 2x2 rib, don't attempt to add or remove any rows until you have completed this.

this against the tension of the pattern that you want to knit.

Altering body length

Looking at it from a very simplistic point of view, is the garment you want to make longer or shorter in the body than the one you have chosen as your ideal fit? This will tell you whether you need to increase or decrease rows from the body of the pattern, using your tension swatch as before.

Does the pattern you want to make have waist shaping? If so, you will need to ensure that this shaping remains in place. If your perfect-fit sweater includes waist shaping, measure how far from the bottom this shaping takes place and make sure that when you add or remove rows, you don't move the waist shaping. By carefully reading the pattern you wish to make, you will be able to see where the waist shaping will fall in comparison with your ideal. Most alterations to body length are best done just above the hem.

Altering the hem width

The number of stitches that you cast on (assuming that you are knitting a bottom-up garment) will determine the width of the bottom of the piece. If the garment is to end around your hips, you might need to customise this for a personal fit. Adding or removing stitches at the cast-on edge will make the bottom of your garment either wider or narrower. Bear in mind that you'll need to make the back and front the same, and that if the garment features an all round lace pattern, you will need to check the stitch repeat before deciding how many

stitches to add or remove. That is, if the lace pattern is 10 stitches wide, there is no use in removing 17 stitches from the cast on because the pattern will then not fit, so go down 20 stitches instead.

Altering sleeve depth

If the measurement from armpit to shoulder is vastly different to that of your ideal garment then you will need to make some amendments. Bear in mind that any rows you add or subtract here will need to be reflected in the sleeve cap shaping, otherwise the two will not fit together.

Look at the other sizes of the pattern. Do they offer a measurement that is closer in fit to the one that you wish to knit? If so, you may be able to use the increases or decreases suggested for the other size on both the sleeve cap and the top of the garment. However, the stitch counts will not match if you do this, so depending on the complexity of the neckline, shoulders and collar, this may lead to more complex alterations being necessary.

Bust measurements

Measure around your actual bust to find out the amount of ease that you have in your ideal-fit garment. If your garment is 3in bigger than your bust size, you need to ensure that the garment you are going to knit is of a similar size.

Most patterns tell you how much ease is given in the pattern, and you should check the actual bust size of the garment rather than the number given 'to fit bust size' so that you can be sure you are making the right size. Compare this with the numbers you have written in your blank schematic and check that you are knitting the right size.

Alter length and width at the hem.

Take care with sleeve caps.

Adjust the bust to fit you.

V-Neck Vest

The deep rib and elegant v-neck make this a stylish layering piece.

Back

Cast on 56 (62, 68, 74, 80, 86, 92) sts.

Row 1: p4, *k3, p3; rep from * to last 4 sts, k4.

Rep Row 1 until rib measures 24cm/9.5in.

Continue in st st until piece measures 31.5 (31.5, 33, 34.5, 35.5, 35.5, 37)cm/12.5 (12.5, 13, 13.5, 14, 14, 14.5)in from cast-on edge, ending with a WS row.

Shape armholes

Cast off 2 (2, 3, 3, 4, 4, 5) sts at beg of next 2 rows. 52 (58, 62, 68, 72, 78, 82) sts.

Continue in st st until piece measures 49.5 (49.5, 52, 54.5, 56, 57, 60)cm/19.5 (19.5, 20.5, 21.5, 22, 22.5, 23.5)in from cast-on edge. Cast off.

Front

Work as for Back until piece measures 34.5 (34.5, 35.5, 37, 38, 38, 39.5)cm/13.5 (13.5, 14, 14.5, 15, 15, 15.5)in from cast-on edge,

ending with a WS row.

Shape neck

Next row (RS): k26 (29, 31, 34, 36, 39, 41), turn. Leave rem sts on holder.

Next row (WS): p2tog, purl to end—1 st dec'd.

Next row (RS): knit.

Rep last 2 rows until 12 (12, 14, 15, 16, 18, 19) sts rem.

Work even, if necessary, until Front measures same as Back to shoulder.

Cast off.

Rejoin yarn to rem sts with RS facing and complete to match first side, reversing shaping.

Finishing

Join shoulder and side seams.

Work 1 round of double crochet around neckline and armholes.

Weave in ends.

About this Pattern...

Yarn Make-up

Manos del Uruguay, Handspun Multicolors (chunky), 100g/126m/138yd, 100% wool

Yarn Alternatives

£   **Save:** Cascade Yarns, Cascade 128

££ **Spend:** Manos del Uruguay Handspun

£££ **Treat:** Rowan, Scottish Aran Tweed

Tension

Work 14 sts and 20 rows to measure 10 x 10cm/4 x 4in over st st. using 5.5mm (US9) needles.

Notions

One pair of 5.5mm (US9) needles

Stitch holder

Crochet hook

Tapestry needle

Size and yarn guide

To fit bust	30–31	32–35	36–38	39–41	42–45	46–48	49–52	in
	76–78.5	81.5–90	91.5–96	99–104	106.5–114.	116.5–122	124.5–132	cm
Actual bust	31	34	37½	41	44.5	48	51.5	in
	78.5	86.5	95	104	113	122	131	cm
Yarn needed								
Jaeger, Extra Fine Merino Chunky 50g/63m/69yd	3 skeins	3 skeins	3 skeins	4 skeins	4 skeins	4 skeins	5 skeins	
Total metres	378	378	378	504	504	504	630	
Total yards	414	414	414	552	552	552	690	

Schematic

15 (16.5, 17.75, 19.5, 20.5, 22, 23.5)in
38 (42, 45, 49.5, 52, 56, 59.5)cm

7 (7, 7.5, 8, 8, 8.5, 9)in
18 (18, 19, 20.5, 20.5, 21.5, 23)cm

12.5 (12.5, 13, 13.5, 14, 14, 14.5)in
31.5 (31.5, 33, 34.5, 35.5, 35.5, 37)cm

15.5 (17, 19, 20.5, 22.25, 24, 25.75)in
39.5 (43, 48.5, 51, 56.5, 61, 65.5)cm

Cable Top

This sleeveless cabled tank uses plant-dyed yarn to make a statement.

About this Pattern...

Yarn Alternatives

£ Save: Sirdar Snuggly 4 ply

££ Spend: Lorna's laces, Shepherd Sock

£££ Treat: Fyberspates, Sparkle Sock

Tension

Work 26 sts and 28 rows to equal 10 x 10cm/4 x 4in in stockinette

Work 32 sts and 28 rows to equal 10 x 10cm/4 x 4in over Cable A pattern

Notions

4.5mm (US 7) circular needle, 60cm/24in long

Tapestry needle

Cable needle

Stitch markers

25mm/1in grosgrain ribbon

Pattern Notes

As this pattern has some very large cable crossings, you may prefer to use a regular double-pointed needle as a cable needle.

Yoke

Cast on 76 (76, 84, 84, 92, 92,100) sts.
Do not join.

Set-up row (RS): K13 (13, 15, 15, 17, 17, 19) (Left Front), pm, k12 (Sleeve), pm, k26 (26, 30, 30, 34, 34, 38) (Back), pm, k12 (Sleeve), pm, k13 (13, 15, 15, 17, 17, 19) (Right Front).

Next row (WS): Purl.

Inc row (RS): *K to 1 st before marker, kfb, sl marker, kfb; rep from * three times more, knit to end. 8 sts inc'd.

Rep the last 2 rows 31 (37, 40, 44, 48, 52, 55) times more, until there are 90 (102, 112, 120, 132, 140, 150) sts in the Back section. Do not turn at end of last row (RS). Join for working in the round.

Divide body and sleeves

Next rnd (RS): K to first marker, cast off all Sleeve sts between first and second markers, k to third marker, cast off all Sleeve sts between third and fourth markers, k to end of rnd.

Next rnd: K across Front to cast-off section, cast on 0 (0, 1, 3, 3, 5,6) sts for underarm, pm for side 'seam', cast on 0 (0, 1, 3, 3, 5, 6) sts for underarm, k across Back to cast-off section, cast on 0 (0, 1, 3, 3, 5, 6) sts for underarm, pm for new beg of round, cast on 0 (0, 1, 3, 3, 5, 6) sts for underarm, k across Front and all the way around Body to beg-of-rnd marker. 180 (204, 228, 252, 276, 300, 324) sts.

Stitch Patterns

Cable A

Worked over 6 sts

Rnds 1–3: Knit.

Rnd 4: *C6L; rep from * to end.

Rnds 5–7: Knit.

Rnd 8: *C6R; rep from * to end.

Rep Rnds 1–8.

Cable B

Worked over 12 sts

Rnds 1–5: Knit.

Rnd 6: C12L.

Rep Rnds 1–6.

Cable C

Worked over 36 sts

Rnds 1–5: Knit.

Rnd 6: (C12L) three times.

Rnds 7–30: Rep Rnds 1–6 four times.

Rnds 31–35: Knit.

Rnd 36: C36L.

Rnds 37–41: Knit.

Rnd 42: C36L.

C6L: Sl 3 sts to cable needle (cn) and hold to front of work, k3, k3 from cn.

C6R: Sl 2 sts to cable needle (cn) and hold to back, k3, k3 from cn.

C12L: Sl 6 sts to cable needle (cn) and hold to front, k6, k6 from cn.

C36L: Sl 18 sts to cable needle (cn) and hold to front, k18, k18 from cn.

Body

Set-up rnd 1: Work Rnd 1 of Cable A 15 (17, 19, 21, 23, 25, 27) times across 90 (102, 114, 126, 138, 150, 162) sts of Front, sl marker, knit across Back to end.

Continue as set with Front sts in Cable A patt and Back in stockinette until you have worked 3 reps (18 rnds total) of Cable A.

Set-up rnd 2: K0 (0, 6, 6, 12, 12, 18) work Rnd 1 of Cable C over next 36 sts, k3 (9, 9, 15, 15, 21, 21), work Rnd 1 of Cable B over next 12 sts, k3 (9, 9, 15, 15, 21, 21), work Rnd 1 of Cable C over next 36 sts, k 0 (0, 6, 6, 12, 12, 18), sl marker, knit across Back to end.

Continue as set with Front sts in est cable patts and Back in stockinette until you have completed the 42 rnds of Cable C.

K 6 rnds, or to desired length.

Cast off.

Finishing

Weave in ends. Allow the stitches at the neck and around the sleeves to roll naturally. Sew the grosgrain ribbon to the inside of the bottom of the garment to prevent it from rolling. If you don't wish to use ribbon, you could work 8 rows of moss stitch, garter stitch or 2x2 rib at the bottom hem before casting off to prevent rolling.

Cable Chart A

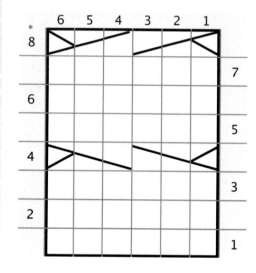

Cable Chart B

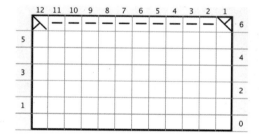

Cable Chart C

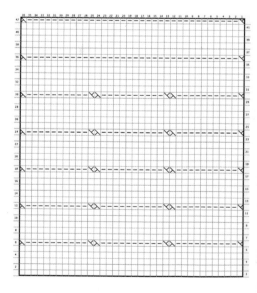

☐ knit
RS: Knit Stitch
WS: Purl Stitch

c3 over 3 left
RS: sl3 to CN, hold to front, K5, K3 from CN

c3 over 3 right
RS: sl3 to CN, hold to back, K3, K3 from CN

c6 over 6 left
RS: sl6 to CN, hold to front, k6, k6 from CN

c18 cover 18 left
RS: sl18 to CN, hold to front, k18, k18 from CN

Shawl-Collar Sweater

This stylish men's sweater is the perfect knit to keep the man in your life warm. The shawl collar is a really nice detail and not as difficult as it looks!

About this Pattern...

Special stitch patterns

Pattern A (in the round)

Rnd 1: Knit.

Rep Rnd 1 for patt.

Pattern A (worked flat)

Row 1 (RS): Knit.

Row 2 (WS): Purl.

Pattern B (in the round)

(worked over 1 st)

Rnd 1: Sl 1 with yarn in back.

Rnd 2: Knit.

Rep Rnds 1–2 for patt.

Pattern B (worked flat)

(worked over 1 st)

Row 1 (RS): Sl 1 with yarn in back.

Row 2: P1.

Pattern C (in the round)

(worked over 30 sts)

Rnds 1–4: P2, k6, p2, k10, p2, k6, p2.

Rnd 5: P2, C6B, p2, C10, p2, C6B, p2.

Rnd 6: P2, k6, p2, k10, p2, k6, p2.

Rep Rnds 1–6 for patt.

Pattern C (worked flat)

(worked over 30 sts) Rows 1 and 3 (RS): P2, k6, p2, k10, p2, k6, p2.

Rows 2 and 4: K2, p6, k2, p10, k2, p6, k2.

Row 5: P2, C6B, p2, C10, p2, C6B, p2.

Row 6: K2, p6, k2, p10, k2, p6, k2.

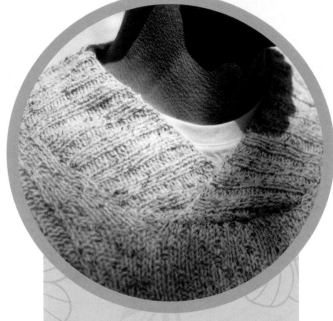

Pattern Notes

Bodice is worked in the round from the hem to the underarm. The sleeves are picked up from the armholes and worked in the round to the cuff.

Special Abbreviations

C6B

Slip 3 sts to cable needle and hold in back, k3, k3 from cable needle.

C10

Slip 4 sts to cable needle and hold in back, slip 2 sts to separate cable needle and hold in front, k4, twist the front cable needle 180-degrees clockwise and knit the 2 sts from cable needle, k4 from back cable needle.

Skills Used

Cables

Working in rows and Rnds

Increasing and decreasing

Pick up and knit

Yarn Used

ColourMart 2/6NM DK • 73% merino, 12% Viscose, 10% silk, 5% cashmere

• 445m/490yd/150g • WPI 14

Colour: Perla Tweed (grey)

Yarn Alternatives

£ **Save:** Coldharbour Mill DK

££ **Spend:** Debbie Bliss Cashmerino DK

£££ **Treat:** Drops Angora Tweed

Tension

Work 20 sts and 30 rows to measure

10 x 10cm or 4 x 4in in stocking stitch using 4mm (US 6) needles, or a size needed to obtain tension.

Notions

A 4mm (US 6) circular needle 80cm/32in long

A 3.5 (US 4) circular needle 80cm/32in long

A set of four 4mm (US 6) double-pointed needles

Two cable needles

Stitch markers

A tapestry needle

Size & yarn amount

Finished chest	99.5	109	119.5	cm
	39	43	47	in
To fit chest	94	104	114.25	cm
	37	41	45	in
Length	66.25	69.75	72.25	cm
	26½	27½	28½	in
Yarn	4	4	5	balls
Total metres	1500	1600	1800	
Total yards	1633	1796	1959	

Pattern D (worked in the round)

(worked over a multiple of 6 sts)

Rnds 1–2: *P1, k5; rep from * to end of round.

Rnd 3–4: *K1, p1, k3, p1; rep from * to end of round.

Rnd 5–6: *K2, p1, k1, p1, k1; rep from * to end of round.

Rnd 7–8: *K3, p1, k2; rep from * to end of round.

Rnd 9–10: *K2, p1, k1, p1, k1; rep from * to end of round.

Rnd 11–12: *K1, p1, k3, p1; rep from * to end of round.

Rep Rnds 1–12 for pattern.

Pattern D (worked flat)

(worked over a multiple of 6 sts)

Row 1: *P1, k5; rep from * to end of row.

Row 2: *P5, k1; rep from * to end of row.

Row 3: *K1, p1, k3, p1; rep from * to end of row.

Row 4: *K1, p3, k1, p1; rep from * to end of row.

Row 5: *K2, p1, k1, p1, k1; rep from * to end of row.

Row 6: *P1, k1, p1, k1, p2; rep from * to end of row.

Row 7: *K3, p1, k2; rep from * to end of row.

Row 8: *P2, k1, p3; rep from * to end of row.

Row 9: *K2, p1, k1, p1, k1 ; rep from * to end of row.

Row 10: *P1, k1, p1, k1, p2; rep from * to end of row.

Row 11: *K1, p1, k3, p1 ; rep from * to end of row.

Row 12: *K1, p3, k1, p1; rep from * to end of row.

Body

With smaller circular needle, cast on 200 (220, 240) sts. Join, be careful not to twist sts. Place a marker at beg of rnd and after 100 (110, 120) sts to mark side seams.

Work 20 rounds in k2, p2 rib. Switch to larger needles. K1 rnd, increasing 20 sts evenly over round. 220 (240, 260) sts, 110 (120, 130) sts each for front and back.

Next rnd: *Patt A 8 (10,12), patt B 1, patt C 30, patt B 1, patt D 30 (36,42), patt B 1, patt C 30, patt B 1, Patt A 8 (10,12); rep from * once more.

Work in est patt until work measures 45.75 (47, 48.25)cm/18 (18.5, 19)in. Move last 110 (120, 130) sts to holder and work Back section on remaining sts.

Back

Next row (RS): Patt A 8 (10,12), patt B 1, patt C 30, patt B 1, patt D 30 (36,42), patt B 1, patt C 30, patt B 1, Patt A 8 (10,12). Turn.

Work flat in established pattern until piece measures 20.5 (22.75, 24)cm/8.5 (9, 9.5)in from armhole. Total length of piece is 66.25 (69.75, 72.25)cm or 26.5 (27.5, 28.5)in. Move remaining sts of back to holder.

Front

Move Front sts to needle and re-attach yarn. Work flat in established pattern for 12 rows.

Next row (RS): Work 45 (50, 55) sts in est patt, cast off 20 sts, work in est patt to end. Working both sides of neck at the same time and attaching a new ball of yarn to the Left Front Neck

On the following row, cont in patt, decreasing 1 st at neck edge every 6th row 5 (6, 7) times. 40 (44, 48) sts rem for each shoulder after decreases are complete.

Work until piece measures same length to shoulders as Back. Keeping centre 30 (32, 34) sts of neck on holders, join shoulders using three-needle cast off.

Sleeves (make 2)

With DPNs, pick up and knit 94 (102, 106) sts around armhole, starting at the beginning of where the front splits from back. Pm and join to work in the rnd.

Rnd 1: Patt A 31 (35, 37), patt B 1, patt C 30, patt B 1, patt A 31 (35, 37).

Cont in patt, decreasing 1 st at each end of rnd (2 sts dec per rnd) every 6 (4, 4) rnds until 60 sts remain. Work even in patt until sleeve measures 38 (40.5, 43.25)cm/15 (16, 17)in. Work in k2, p2 rib for another 7.5cm/3in.

Cast off all sts.

Shawl collar

With larger circular needle, and making sure that the total number of sts picked up is evenly divisible by 4, pick up and knit 2 sts for every 3 rows up front right neck, knit all held sts from back neck, pick up and knit 2 sts for every 3 rows down front left neck.

Do not join.

Turn.

Work in k2, p2 rib until work measures 11.5cm/4.5in.

Cast off all stitches.

Finishing

Weave in ends.

Sew sides of collar down to centre front neck cast off sts, making sure that the left side of collar overlaps the right side.

Block to measurements.

This yarn feels stiff at first, but it softens greatly when you work with it. There is enough elasticity in it to work cables.

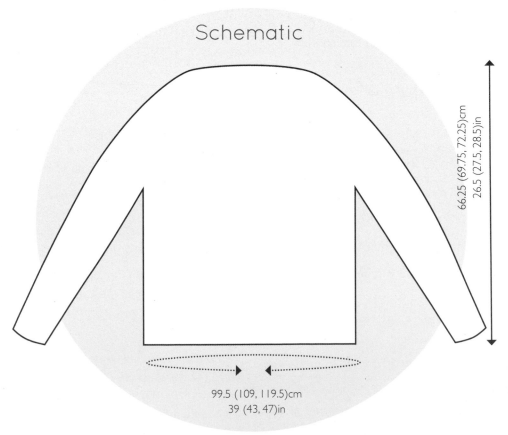

Schematic

66.25 (69.75, 72.25)cm
26.5 (27.5, 28.5)in

99.5 (109, 119.5)cm
39 (43, 47)in

Buttoned Cardigan

This wonderful cables-and-seed stitch gives it a classic look that will look great on any man.

Special stitch patterns

This pattern contains a chart

Pattern notes

Seed stitch:

Row 1: k1: p1 (repeat)

Row 2: knit as sts appear in front of you

Row 3: p1: k1 (repeat)

Row 4: knit as sts appear in front of you

Pattern starts
Lower Body

Cast on with 3.0 mm needles:
220–240–260 sts.

Place markers:

S: 55–110–55

M: 60–120–60

L: 65–130–65

Ribbing:

Work 20 rows in k2 p2 rib.

Continue:

Knit 1 row

Purl 1 row

Divide for pattern

Front left and right

Small: 11 sts A: 34 sts B: 10 sts A
Middle: 13 sts A: 34 sts B: 13 sts A
Large: 16 sts A: 34 sts B: 15 sts A

Front left and right

Small: 11 sts A: 34 sts B: 10 sts A
Middle: 13 sts A: 34 sts B: 13 sts A
Large: 16 sts A: 34 sts B: 15 sts A

For the back

Small: 11 sts A: 34 sts B: 20 sts A: 34 sts B: 11 sts A

Middle: 13 sts A: 34 sts B: 26 sts A: 34 sts B: 13 sts A

Large: 16 sts A: 34 sts B: 30 sts A: 34 sts B: 16 sts A

A: Seed stitch

B: Chart over 34 sts

Work in pattern scheme until a length of 38 – 40 – 42cm/15–15.7–16.5in is reached.

From here the parts are knit separate.

Tension

Work 28 st and 36 rows in seed stitch
st to measure 10 x 10cm/4 x 4in using
3mm needles, or size required to obtain tension.

About this Pattern...

Skills Used

Decreasing

Pick up and knit / Pick up and purl

Knitting in the round

Knitting in rows

Working from a chart

Measurements

Small, Middle and Large:

Small: from bottom to shoulder: 58cm/22.8in

from bottom to armpit 38cm/15in

Middle: from bottom to armpit: 40cm/15.7in

from bottom to shoulder: 62cm/24.4in

Large: from bottom to armpit 42cm/16.5in

from bottom to shoulder 66cm/26in

Sleeve length: 50cm/19.6in for all sizes

Yarn Used

ColourMart 2–15mm 100% wool – 770 yards per 150 grams – colour 34
(Navy) You need 2 cones of 150 grams
for each size.
Approx needed:
Small: 875–950m/800–850yd
Middle: 950–985m/850–900yd
Large: 985–1040m/900–950yd

Right front

Work over the first 55–60–65 sts: (start with right side in front) Work in pattern. Decrease for V-neck shape:

SSK (stitch 1 and 2) in row 5–11–17 (repeat until total height is reached)

These decreases fall together with the rows in which you need to cable.

Cast off sts when a total length of 58–62–66cm/22.8–24.4–26in is reached.

Back

Work over 110 –120–130 sts: (start with right side in front) Work in pattern. Cast off sts when a total length of 58–62–66cm/22.8–24.4–26in is reached.

Left front

Work over the remaining 55–60–65 sts, (Start with right side in front).

K2tog the last two sts, in row 5–11–17 (repeat until total height is reached).

These decreases fall together with the rows in which you need to cable.

Cast off sts when a total length of 58–62–66cm/22.8–24.4–26in is reached.

Shoulders

Sew from arm to neck: the first 34–36–39 sts. Secure and weave in ends.

Key

Cable over 6 sts: Place 3 on cable needle in front of your work, knit 3, knit 3 from cable needle.

Cable over 6 sts: Place 3 on cable needle at the back of your work, knit 3, knit 3 from cable needle.

Cable over 4 sts: Place 1st on cable needle at back of your work, knit 3, purl 1 from cable needle.

Cable over 4 sts: Place 3sts on cable needle in front of your work, purl 1, knit 3 from cable needle.

Twist 6 st: Place 6 st on cable needle, twist counter clockwise 180°, knit sts from cable needle.

Cable over 3 sts: Place 2 st on cable needle in front of work, purl 1, knit 2 from cable needle.

Cable over 2 sts: Pace 1 st on cable needle in front of work, purl 1, knit 1 from cable needle.

Cable over 3 sts: Place 1 on cable needle at the back of work, knit 2, purl 1 from cable needle.

Cable over 2 sts: Place 1st on cable needle in front of work, knit1, purl 1 from cable needle.

Sleeves

Worked in the round. Start in armpit – with needles 3mm, pick up 92–96–100 sts. Mark the beginning point of your round. Work in pattern A (seed stitch)

Decrease however in every 10th round: 2 x 1 st repeat these decreases another 7 times (8 times in total)

Work in the round until a total arm length of 45 cm is reached. Switch to 2.5 mm needles.

Ribbing

k2 p2 rib for 5cm/2in. Cast off sts. Work second sleeve.

Border: Right front

Work in rows:

With right side in front: Pick up sts for border over a length of 38–40–42cm/ 15–15.7–16.5in [direction: bottom to armplt] (76–80–84 st) Turn.

Border: Left front

Work in rows: With right side in front: Pick up sts for border over a length of 38–40–42cm/15–15.7–16.5in [direction: armpit to bottom] (76–80–84 st)

Turn.

Work rows in k2, p2 rib: 4 rows

Row 5: k2, p2.

Make button holes: for all sizes:

Sts: 3 + 4, 15 + 16, 27 + 28, 39 + 40, 51 + 52, 63 + 64, p2tog, Yo, Yo.

Row 6: Continue to work in k2, p2 rib – drop the extra YO.

Row 7 – 10: Work in k2 p 2 rib. Cast off sts loosely.

Neckline

Start on right front: Pick up sts along the neckline to the left front. (128 – 136 – 144 st) Turn. Work in k2, p2 rib for 5 rows.

Cast off sts loosely.

Weave in all ends. Sew buttons.

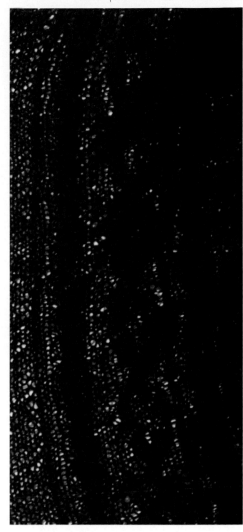

Chart

The chart spans columns 34 (left) to 1 (right) and rows 1 (bottom) to 20 (top), showing knitting symbols.

Little Shrug

This pretty little lace shrug is the perfect way to use up a bit of very lovely yarn.

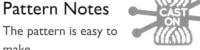

Pattern Notes

The pattern is easy to make
longer if you have more yarn –
simply increase the lace section for the arms.

Pattern starts: Sleeve 1

Cast on 57 (57, 63, 63, 67, 67, 73, 73, 79, 79) stitches and work 4 rows in garter stitch.

*Row 1 (RS): (K2tog, yo) to last st, k1.

Row 2: Purl.

Rep last 2 rows 35 (35, 43, 43, 49, 49, 57, 57, 63, 63) times more.**

Back

Work 92 (100, 104, 108, 112, 118, 120, 126, 138, 148) rows in st st.

Sleeve 2

Rep from * to ** for second sleeve.

Work 4 more rows in garter st.

Cast off.

Finishing

Sew up sleeve seams.

Press and block to measurements.

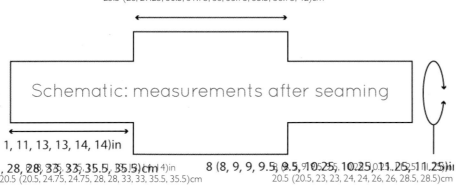

10 (11, 11.5, 12, 12.5, 13, 13.25, 14, 15.25, 16.5)in
25.5 (28, 29.25, 30.5, 31.75, 33, 33.75, 35.5, 38.75, 42)cm

Schematic: measurements after seaming

1, 11, 13, 13, 14, 14)in

, 28, 28, 33, 33, 35.5, 35.5)cm 4)in
20.5 (20.5, 24.75, 24.75, 28, 28, 33, 33, 35.5, 35.5)cm

8 (8, 9, 9, 9.5, 9.5, 10.25, 10.25, 11.25, 11.25)in
20.5 (20.5, 23, 23, 24, 24, 26, 26, 28.5, 28.5)cm

Size and yarn amount

To fit age	1	2	3	4	5	6	7	8	9	10	years
To fit chest	18.5	20	21	22	23	24	25	26	28.5	30	in
	47	51	54	56	58	61	63	66	72	78	cm
Length	17	18	20	20.5	22.5	23	25	25.5	28.5	29.5	in
	43.5	45.5	51	52	57	58.5	63.5	65	72	75	cm

Girls' Striped Cardigan

This cool cardigan would make a lovely addition to any girl's wardrobe, its nautical style appealing to little tomboys and budding fashionistas alike.

Body

Cast on 138 (158, 168, 188) sts.

PM after 34 (40, 42, 47) sts and 104 (118, 126, 141) sts to mark side 'seams.' Begin stripe pattern and work in st st throughout. Continue in stocking stitch until work measures 14 (15.25, 16.5, 17.75) cm/5.5 (6, 6.5, 7)in, ending with a WS row.

Work eyelet row: K0 (0, 2, 2), (K2, yo, k2tog) to last 2 (2, 4, 4) sts, k2 (2, 4, 4).

Purl 1 row.

Continuing in st st and with the stripe pattern as set, shape front edge by working the decrease row on the next and following fourth row 10 times as follows:

Decrease row: K2, k2tog, k to last 4 sts, k2togtbl, k2.

116 (136, 146, 166) sts remain. 23 (29, 31, 36) sts before first marker and after third marker.

Work even in patt until work measures 30.5 (33, 35.5, 38)cm/12 (13, 14, 15)in ending with a WS row. Shape armholes by splitting work as follows.

Right front

Knit to first marker, remove marker and turn and work on these stitches.

Cast off 3 stitches at beginning of row and then work even in st st and stripe patt until armhole measures, 5 (6.5, 7.5, 7.5)

cm/2 (2, 3, 3)in ending with a WS row. 20 (26, 28, 33) sts.

Leave sts on a holder and rejoin yarn to main piece of work at Back with RS facing.

Back

Cast off 3 sts, k to next marker.

Remove marker and turn and work on these sts.

Cast off 3 stitches at beg of next row. 66 (72, 78, 88) sts.

Continue in st st and working stripe pattern as set until work measures 5 (6.5, 7.5, 7.5) cm/2 (2.5, 3, 3)in, ending with a WS row.

Leave stitches on a holder and rejoin yarn to main piece of work.

About this Pattern...

Skills Used
Decreasing
Working stripes
Pick up and knit

Yarns Used
Rowan Amy Butler Belle Organic DK 50% Organic Wool, 50% Organic Cotton, 50g/120m/131yd
MC: Indigo, Colour No. 001
CC: Moon

Yarn Alternatives

£   **Save:** Rico Lifestyle

££ **Spend:** Rowan Wool Cotton

£££ **Treat:** Sublime Baby Cashmere Merino Silk K

Tension
Work 22 sts and 30 rows to measure 10 x 10cm/4 x 4in in stocking stitch using 4mm (US 6) needles or size needed to obtain gauge.

Notions
A pair of 4mm (US 6) needles
Stitch markers
Tapestry needle

Special Stitch Patterns
Stripe pattern
Work 6 rows in MC.
Work 6 rows in CC.

Special Abbreviations
m: marker
sm: slip marker

Left front

Cast off 3 stitches and knit to end. Continue to work in st st and stripe patt, until armhole measures 5 (6.5, 7.5, 7.5)cm/2 (2½, 3, 3)in ending with a WS row. 20 (26, 28, 33) sts.

Shape raglan

Turn and purl across Left Front, PM, cast on 17 (19, 21, 23) sts for sleeve, PM, purl across Back sts, PM, cast on 17 (19, 21, 23) sts for sleeve, PM, purl across Right Front. 140 (162, 176, 200) sts.

Shape Raglan, cont in stripe patt as follows.

Next row (RS): *K to 2 sts before m, k2tog, sm, k2tog; rep from * three times more, k to end.

Next row (WS): *P to 2 sts before m, p2tog, sm, p2tog; rep from * three times more, p to end.

Rep last 2 rows 6 (7, 8, 9) times more.

28 (34, 32, 40) sts rem.

Next row (RS): *K to 2 sts before m, ssk, sm, k3tog, sm, k2tog; rep from * once more, k to end. 20 (26, 22, 32) sts rem.

Work even until the next stripe of colour is completed and cast off all sts.

Finishing

Pick up and knit 3 sts for every 4 rows along the left edge and then cast off without knitting a row.

Repeat for other side and around armholes.

Cut 2 lengths of yarn (one in each colour) that are approx 2m/2yd long. Twist to make a 2-colour cord and thread through the eyelets to fasten.

Schematic

43.25 (47, 50.75, 54)cm/17 (18.5, 20, 21.25)in

30.5 (33, 35.5, 38)cm 12 (13, 14, 15)in

14 (15.25, 16.5, 17.75)cm 5.5 (6, 6.5, 7)in

12.75 (14, 15.25, 16)cm/5 (5.5, 6, 6.25)in

66.5 (73, 77.5, 87)cm 25 (28.75, 30.5, 34.25)in

The fresh nautical stripes and luscious cotton-blend yarn give this cardigan a classic, timeless feel.

Size and yarn amount

Age	7–8	9–10	11–12	13–14	years
Finished chest	25	28½	30½	34	in
	66	72	78	87	cm
Length	17	18½	20	21¼	in
	43.25	47	50.75	54	cm
Yarn (MC) balls	3	4	4	5	
Total metres	360	480	480	600	
Total yards	393	524	524	655	
Yarn (CC) balls	3	4	4	5	
Total metres	360	480	480	600	
Total yards	393	524	524	655	

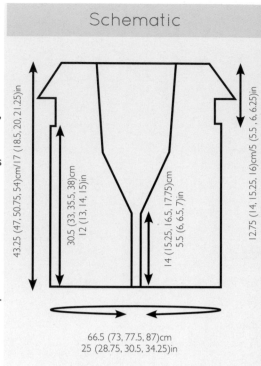

Pattern Notes

The bottom of this cardigan is supposed to roll organically – if you would prefer this to be more structured, you should work 4 rows of garter stitch before beginning the pattern as set.

Accessories

This section contains delightful accessories to jazz up your outfits or be given as gifts. Try out some new techniques and produce heartfelt, home-made items.

Pretty in Pink

This gorgeous, delicate knit is perfect for cool summer evenings and looks sensational in pretty pastel pink.

3
ADVANCED

About this Pattern...

Pattern starts

Cabled Centre Panel

With 3mm needles cast on:
42 + 2 = 44 sts.

Knit 1 row, turn

Reversed Stocking Stitch

Row 1 (rs): Sl1p, purl to end, turn

Row 2 (ws): Sl1p knit to end, turn

Row 3–6: Repeat row 1 and 2

Pattern Block: Turn at the end of every row

Row 1: Sl1p, p6, k30, p7

Row 2: Sl1k, k6, p30, k7

Row 3: rep row 1

Row 4: rep row 2

Row 5: Sl1p, p6, C6B, five times, p7

Row 6: rep row 2

Row 7 & 9: rep row 1

Row 8 & 10: rep row 2

Row 11: Sl1p, p6, k3 C6F four times, k3, p7

Row 12: Rep row 2

Work rows 1–12 an additional nine times

(120 rows in total)

Work row 1–6 once.

Work 6 rows in Reversed st st.

Special stitch patterns

Sl1p Slip 1 as if to purl

Sl1k Slip 1 as if to knit

C6F (Cable 6 Front) slip the next 3sts onto cable needle, place the cable needle at the front of the work, K next 3sts from left needle, K 3sts from cable needle

C6B (Cable 6 Back) slip the next 3sts onto cable needle, place the cable needle at the back of the work, k next 3sts from left needle, k 3sts from cable needle

Skills Used

Decreasing
Lace
Cables
Pick up and knit/purl
Working from a chart

Measurements

Blocked length
2.67m x 59cm/3yd x 23yd

Yarn Used

Adriafil Zephir 50 Classic
Colour 04
1 skein
50% wool, 50% acrylic
100g/1200m/1312yd
cobweb 1 ply

Yarn Alternatives

£ Save: ClourMart Cashmere/
      Wool 1/28nm

££ Spend: Wharfdale Woolworks

£££ Treat: Posh Yarn Miranda
      Cobweb

Tension

Work 20st and 40 rows in st st to measure 10 x 10cm/4 x 4in using 3mm needles, or size required to obtain tension.

Notions

Circular or long straight needles:
3mm and 4.5mm
Cable needle 2.5mm
Stitch marker
Thread and needle to add lifelines

Left side panel

Pick up 75sts along the left side of the cable panel (right side uppermost). Turn. Purl 1 row. Turn.

Work pattern chart A

Pattern is worked over 15 sts and should be repeated five times to finish the row.

Work row 1–20 five times (100 rows total)

Row 101–120: work pattern A four times, work pattern chart B once

Row 121–140: work pattern A three times, work pattern B once

Row 141–160: work pattern A two times, work pattern B once

Row 161–180: work pattern A once, work pattern B once

Row 181–199: Work pattern B row 1–19

Row 200: Separately given under pattern chart B

Cast off left panel.

Right side panel

Pick up 75 sts along the right side of the cable panel (right side uppermost). Turn. Purl 1 row. Turn

Work pattern chart A

Pattern is worked over 15 sts and should be repeated five times to finish the row.

Work rows 1–20 five times (100 rows in total)

Row 101–120: work pattern C once, work pattern A four times

Row 121–140: work pattern C once, work pattern A three times

Row 141–160: work pattern C once, work pattern A two times

Row 161–180: work pattern C once, work pattern A once

Row 181–199: work pattern C row 1–19.

Row 200: Separately given under pattern chart C

Cast off right panel.

Border

Starting at the left panel: Pick up stitches around the bottom of the shawl. Turn. (approximately 420 sts)

Row 1: Knit all sts. Turn

Row 2: Sl1k, *yo, k1 (repeat from * to end), turn

Row 3: Sl1k, knit all sts and drop yo

Row 4: repeat row 2

Row 5: repeat row 3

Rows 6 & 7: repeat row 1

Cast off loosely, using: k1, *yo, pass st on right needle over yo, k1, pass stitch over (repeat from *)

Top border

With right side of shawl uppermost – starting on the right-hand side, pick up stitches over the entire length of the shawl. Turn. Work five rows in garter stitch. Cast off. Weave in ends. Block shawl.

Charts

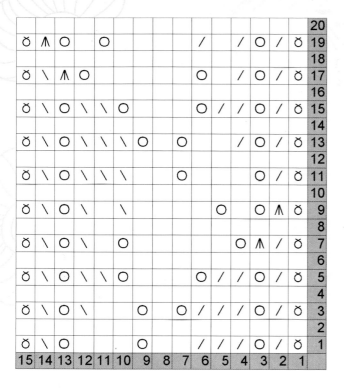

Chart A

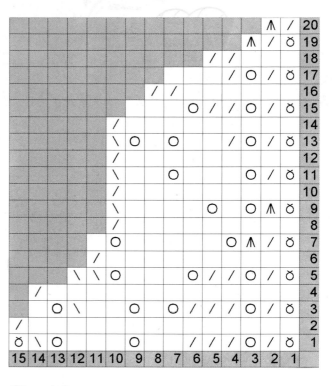

Chart B

Row 200 for chart B

Row 200 for chart C

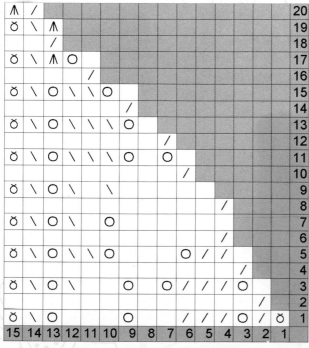

Chart C

⋀	double decrease
\	SSK
/	k2tog
ŏ	make back loop
O	yarn over
	knit on right side, purl on wrong side
	no stitch

Stylish Wristwarmer

These adorable wristwarmers are the perfect project for those looking to improve their skills. Try a range of colours to match different outfits.

2
INTERMEDIATE

About this Pattern...

Pattern notes

The chart that you choose to use should be in the region of 18 rows high and either 44 stitches wide or a number that can be divided by 44. If you wanted to use a chart that was 10 stitches wide you could either add in some plain stitches either side or decrease the number of stitches to 40.

If you want to turn this design into fingerless gloves you would simply knit them longer and either knit them flat and seam together leaving a space for your thumb or you could cast off a large buttonhole for your thumb to go through if you want to knit them in the round. Or why not use this as a good opportunity to try a steek?

Pattern starts

Cast on 44 stitches using solid yarn and join to work in round. Work in 2 x 2 rib for 15 rounds. Continue in stocking stitch for 2 rounds. Switch to a 2 round solid and 2 round multicoloured yarn stripe pattern and work 18 rounds in stocking stitch in total. Continue in multicoloured yarn and work 1 round of eyelets as below:

(K2tog YO) Repeat to last 2 stitches, K2tog

Work 2 more rounds in stocking stitch.

Cast off.

Finishing

Fold over and sew the picot/eyelet row in place so that the picots are on top of the hand.

Skills Used
Knitting in the round
YOs

Finished Measurements
15 x 12cm / 5.9 x 4.7in

Yarns Used
Colinette Cadenza DK - Bright Charcoal Rowan Wool DK - Grey Oddments of each

Yarn Alternatives
£ **Save:** Wendy Bliss Merini

££ **Spend:** Debbie Bliss Rialto DK

£££ **Treat:** Fibre Company - Acadia

Tension
18 stitches and 24 rows to 10cm over stocking stitch using 4.5mm needles

Notions
4.5mm DPNs or circulars
Darning needle

Top Tip

Wristwarmers are the
perfect canvas for
experimenting as they
are small and quick
to knit.

Tunia Scarf

This lovely piece will take you from summer through to autumn.

2
INTERMEDIATE

About this Pattern...

This beautiful pattern is simple to knit and shows off variegated yarns beautifully. The stitch pattern creates a natural bias shape to the fabric and just 1 skein of sock yarn makes a super long scarf that can be wrapped around your neck or left to hang down. You could use any hand-painted yarn for this project, just make sure that the needle size is appropriate to the weight of the yarn.

Bias Eyelet Pattern

Multiple of 2 sts

Row 1 (WS): Purl.

Row 2 (RS): K1, *YO, k2tog; rep from * to last st, k1.

Rep Rows 1–2 for pattern.

Pattern

Cast on 30 sts. Work in Bias Eyelet Pattern for 118" [300 cm], or to desired length, ending with a WS row.

Bind off.

Finishing

Weave in ends. Block.

Finished Measurements

Approx 15 x 300cm/6 x 118in

Yarn

1 skein HipKnits sock yarn

Tension

Work 22 sts and 30 rows to measure
4 x 4in, 10 x 10cm Bias Eyelet Pattern

Notions

US 7 [4.5 mm] straight needles
Tapestry needle